COLLAGE
HEAVEN
WWW.COLLAGEHEAVEN.COM

MW00876914

THE CUT OUT & COLLAGE BOOK

600+

AMAZING THINGS TO CUT & COLLAGE

DOWNLOAD INCLUDED

BOOK CONTENT

INTRODUCTION

Collage art is a technique where various materials such as paper, fabric, photographs, and found objects are arranged and glued together to create a new artwork. It's a form of mixed media art that allows the artist to explore new possibilities and create a unique visual language. To create a collage, you will need a few basic tools:

 to cut paper, fabric, or other materials into various shapes and sizes.

SCISSORS

 to measure and cut straight line

RULER

 to adhere the materials together. A glue stick or double-sided tape can also be used.

GLUE

 to sketch out ideas and make placement marks

PENCIL

CUTTING MAT to protect your work surface and make cutting easier.

Message From:

We have recently seen a number of complaints from our valued customers regarding the pricing of some of our books. We understand and regret any confusion or dissatisfaction caused by the higher price point. As an independent author on Amazon KDP, we have had to make the difficult decision to reduce the size of the bigger graphics to minimize the number of pages in our book in order to make it more affordable for our readers. This was necessary in order to incorporate more premium images and high-quality paper, while still being able to offer competitive pricing through Amazon's handling of the shipping and printing of the book. We are grateful for your support of our small business and want to thank you for choosing to purchase our book through Amazon. As a token of our appreciation, we have included a free download of the book in high-quality print format.
Thank you for your understanding and continued support.

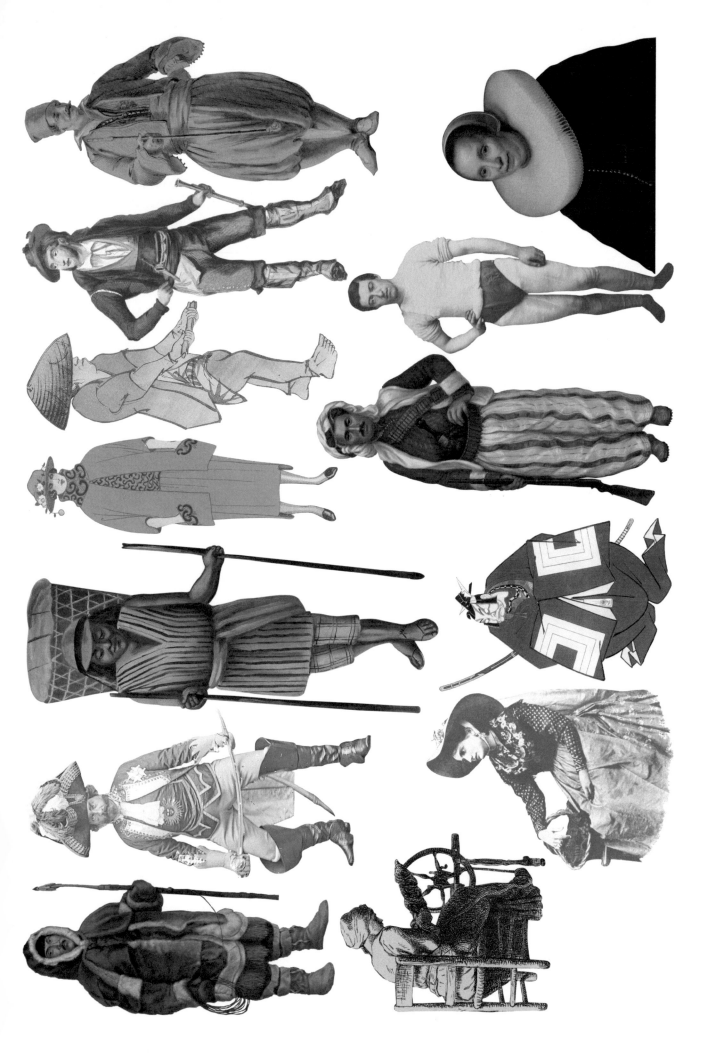

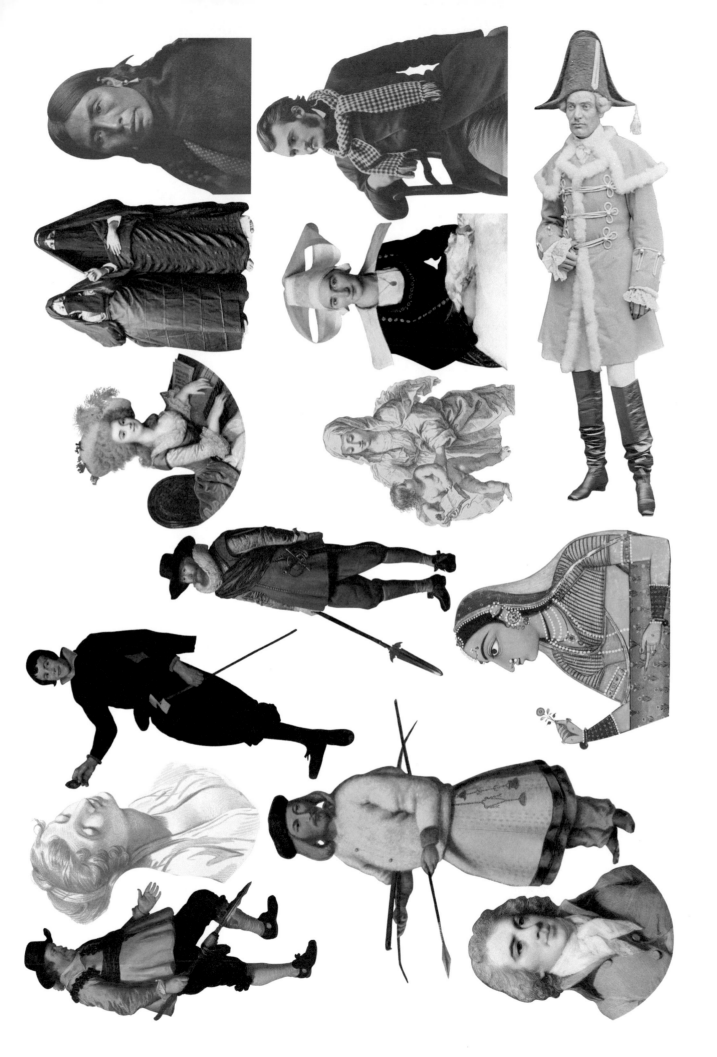

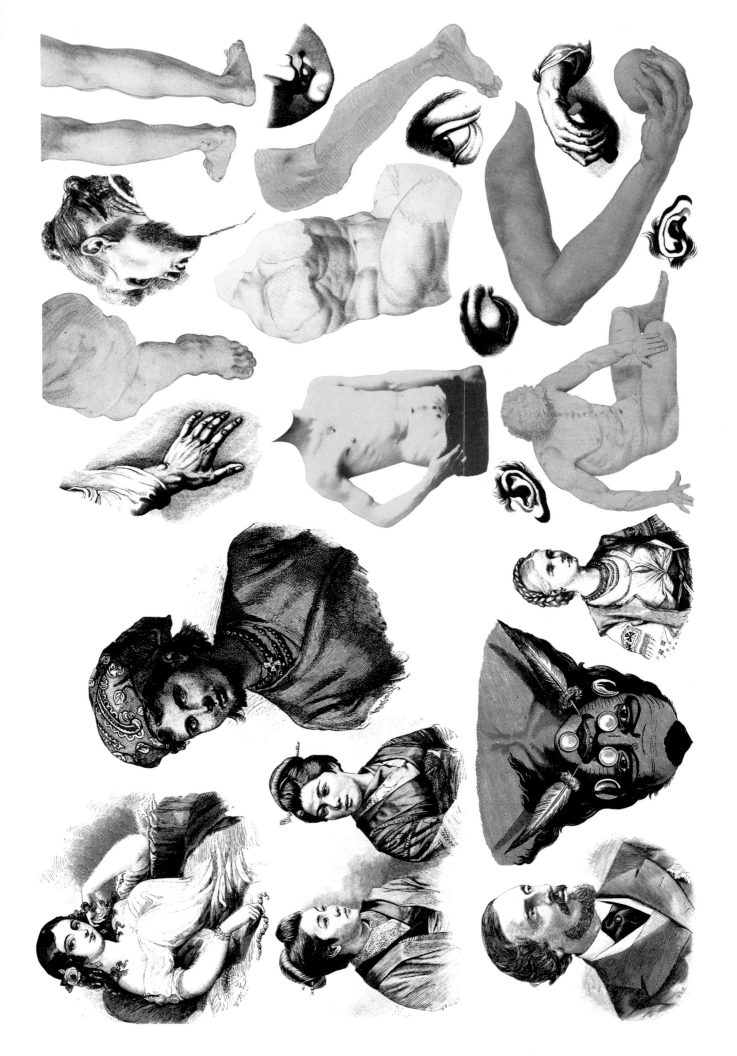

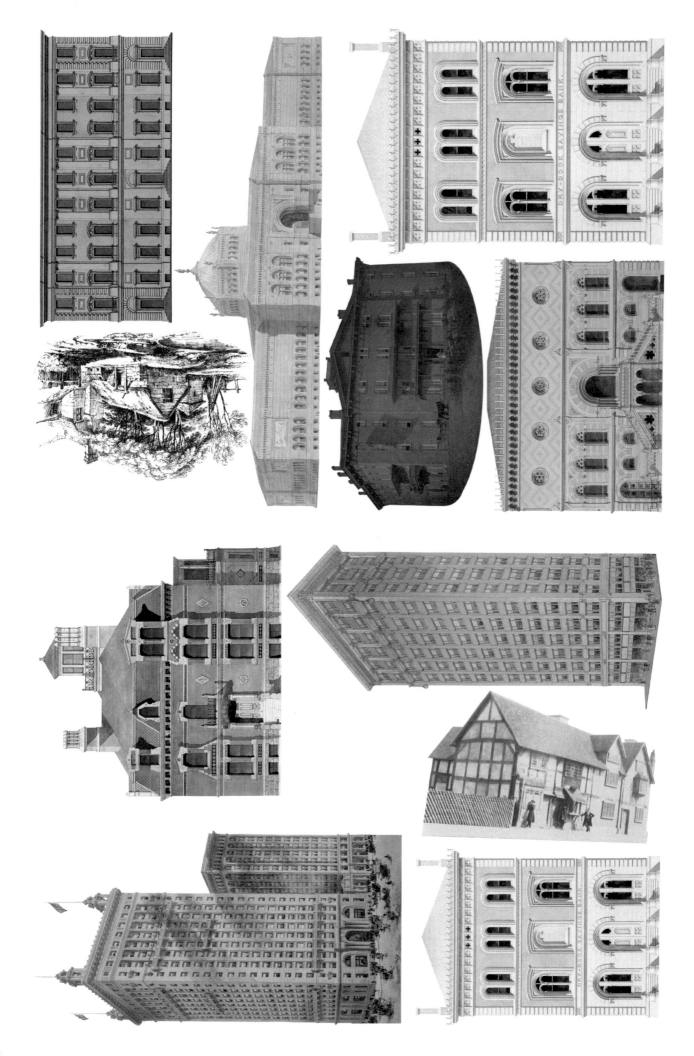

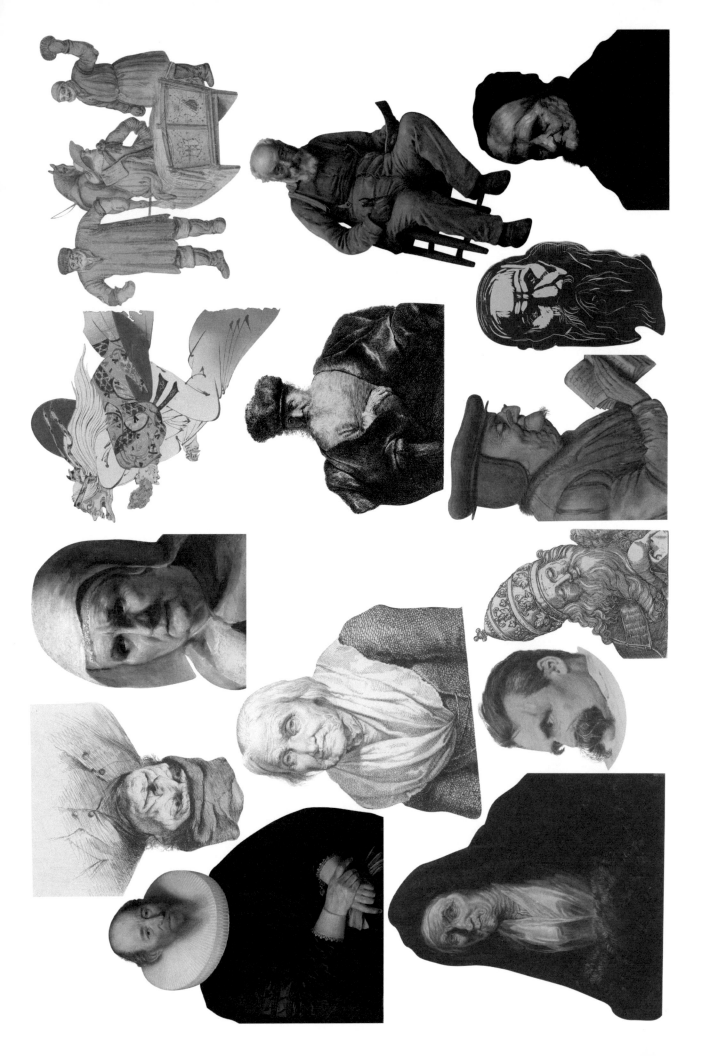

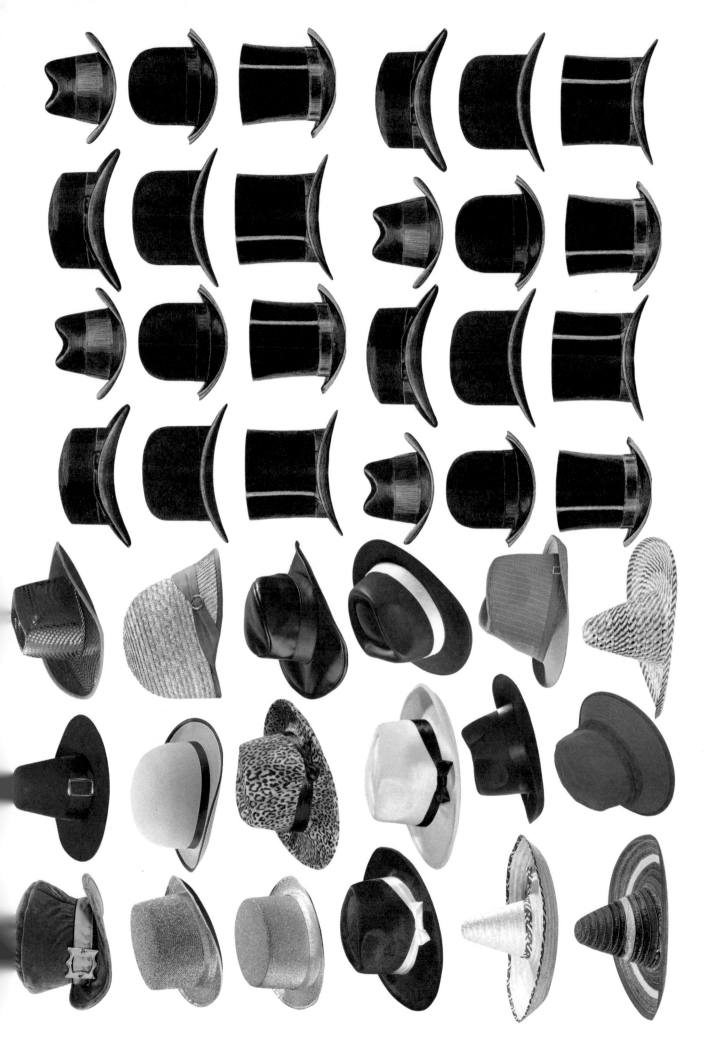

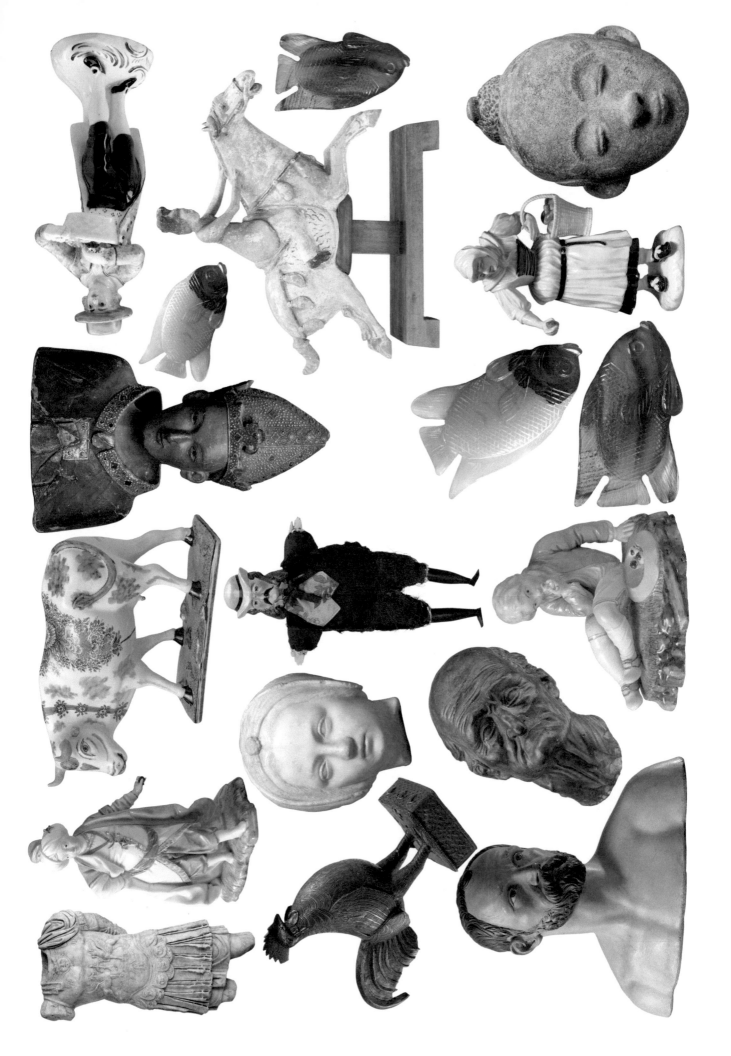

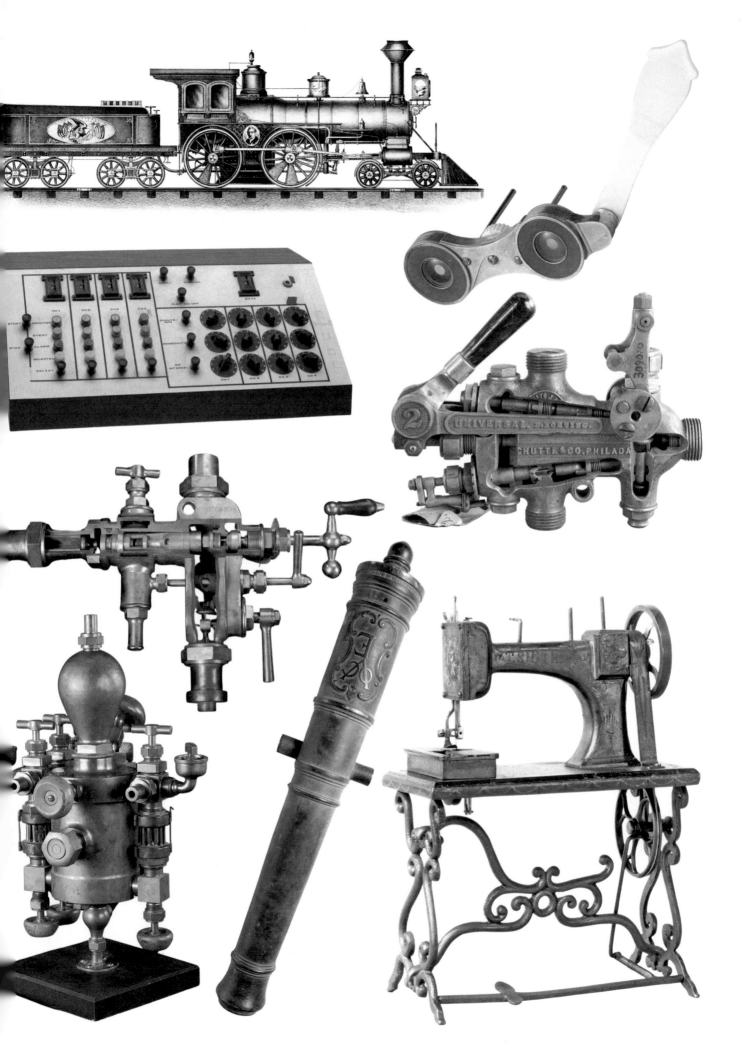

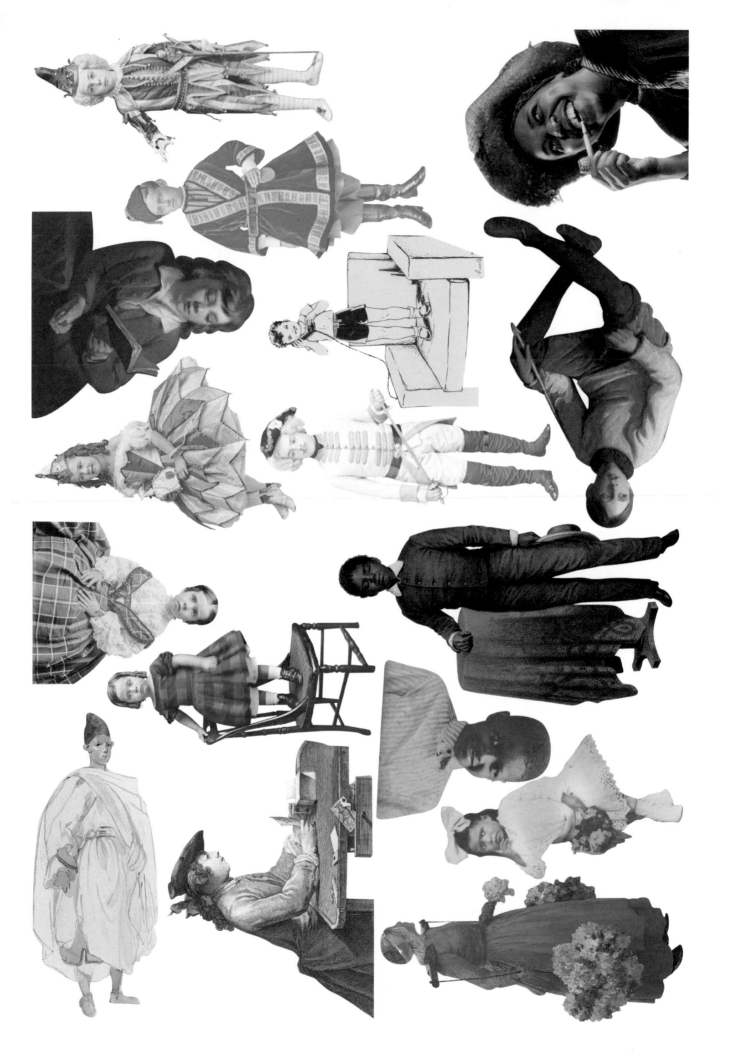

FREE COLLAGE SHEETS

DOWNLOAD YOUR FREE COLLAGE SHEETS

VISIT:

WWW.COLLAGEHEAVEN.COM/B/600ELEMENTS

SCAN ME

ZIP FILE PASSWORD:

mPagjZv!#Tzw8k3E

Our Other Published
Books Titles
www.collageheaven.com

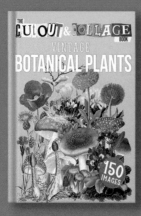

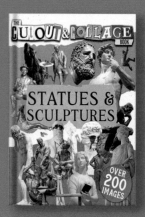

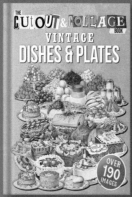

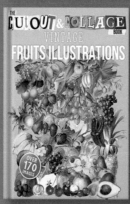

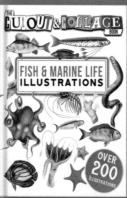

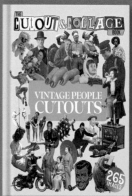

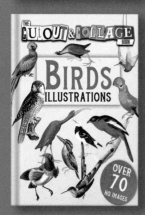

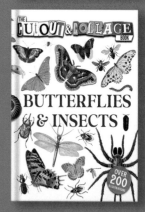

Leave us a Comment:

WE'D LOVE TO HEAR YOUR HONEST OPINION

★★★★★

Made in United States
Troutdale, OR
11/19/2023